I See You, and I Know!

G_d's All-Seeing Eye and Inescapable Presence

(2nd Ed.)

SHEILA G. BULLOCK

Copyright © 2024 Sheila G. Bullock

All rights reserved. No part of this book may be reproduced, stored, or transmitted by any means—whether auditory, graphic, mechanical, or electronic—without written permission of both publisher and author, except in the case of brief excerpts used in critical articles and reviews. Unauthorized reproduction of any part of this work is illegal and is punishable by law.

ISBN: 979-8-89419-185-0 (sc)
ISBN: 979-8-89419-186-7 (hc)
ISBN: 979-8-89419-187-4 (e)

Because of the dynamic nature of the Internet, any web addresses or links contained in this book may have changed since publication and may no longer be valid. The views expressed in this work are solely those of the author and do not necessarily reflect the views of the publisher, and the publisher hereby disclaims any responsibility for them.

One Galleria Blvd., Suite 1900, Metairie, LA 70001
(504) 702-6708

All Scripture quotations, unless otherwise indicated, are taken from:

The Woman's Study Bible
Copyright© 1995 by Thomas Nelson, Inc.

The Holy Bible, New King James Version
Copyright© 1982 by Thomas Nelson, Inc.

The New King James Bible, New Testament
Copyright© 1979 by Thomas Nelson, Inc.

The New King James Bible, New Testament and Psalms
Copyright© 1980 by Thomas Nelson, Inc.

Other Scripture references are from the following sources:

King James Version (KJV) by Public Domain, Biblegateway.com.

English Standard Version (ESV)
The Holy Bible, English Standard Version Copyright© 2001 by Crossing Bibles, a publishing ministry of Good News Publishers.

New Living Translation (NLT)

New International Version (NIV)
Holy Bible, New International Version®
NIV® Copyright© 1973, 1978, 1984, 2011 by Biblica, Inc.®
Used by permission. All rights reserved worldwide.

The Amplified Bible®, (AB) Copyright© 1987 by the Zondervan Corporation and the Lockman Foundation.

This book is dedicated to my L-RD and Savior, Jesus Christ, who has allowed me to experience the joys of being a girl, teenager, daughter, sister, wife, aunt, mother, friend, grandmother, minister, and a first lady;

For all who will read with an open mind
to allow our Heavenly Father to
Speak into their life and
for the family of my dear friend, the Late E.S. Robertson.
I truly miss you.

G-d loves you, He sees and He knows!

CONTENTS

Foreword ix
Reflections xi
Acknowledgments xxvii
Special Acknowledgement xxix
Precious Memories xxx
To All Readers xxxii
Prologue xxxiii

Chapter 1   G-d Knows Your Name 1
Chapter 2   G-d Knows Where You Sit 12
Chapter 3   G-d Knows When You Rise 24
Chapter 4   G-d Understands Your Thoughts 31
Chapter 5   G-d Hands Are Upon Me! 40
Chapter 6   You Cannot Escape! 48
Chapter 7   I Give Up! 56
Chapter 8   Search Me Out 63
Chapter 9   Lead Me 69

Epilogue 79
Endnotes 85
About the Author 89

FOREWORD

Our Almighty God is amazing – always revealing Himself to those who desire to know Him more intimately. Only a person who has spent time in His presence can experience the true character of the love and concern He has for human mankind. The Omniscient Father longs for His children to come to Him without doubt or hesitation. The more we learn of Him, we will transition into another level of trusting Him in all things.

This book is not for casual inquirers, but for those who can hear and perceive that "I See You, and I Know!" One must let go of past failures, past hurts, past doubts and all contrary philosophies in order to grasp the fact that God is knowledgeable of the depth, breath, and height of life's troublesome situations. The incomparable Father is always in control and answers to the cry of the righteous.

From this book, you will deeply understand and appreciate Our Heavenly Father who knows you better than yourself. He is touched with the feelings of your infirmities. He utters from His heart, "I See You, and I Know".

Enjoy the read!

Evang. Regina Gainer – *Executive Pastor*
Christ Temple Ministries

Author, Fight or Die!
Securely Positioned and
Hello, My Name is Josephine

REFLECTIONS

As Sheila Bullock's husband and Pastor, I fully endorse her work but G-d has placed His approval upon her ministry. This book is the result of many prayers, tears, and hard work and gives you an account of real life experiences. The reading of this book will give you strength and encouragement to know you are never alone in your walk through life. The reading will give you hope and comfort as you cope with everyday life's issues. Congratulations Sheila for an inspirational guidance that will move a person from a place of frustration and isolation towards G-d's All-Seeing Eye and Inescapable Presence, "I See You and I Know!"

Rev. Nathaniel Bullock, Jr., ThB
Pastor, Founder and President
New Life Community Development Corporation

It is with great honor to be asked to share reflections on this latest addition to Minister Sheila Bullock's series of devotionals for the believer in Christ. Minister Bullock has committed her life to serving God's people with her multi-gifted talents and love for God.

This latest published work will surely be a blessing to all that read and meditated on what God has led Minister Bullock to share with us. As her Pastor and Bishop, my prayer is as she has been a blessing to me, may through this latest work be a blessing to you.

From the Desk of Bishop, Dr. Ronald L. Owens
New Hope Baptist Church

When I first met Minister Sheila, I immediately fell in love with her. She exuded so much compassion and concern for what she was doing. The next time I had the opportunity to speak with her, she demonstrated a nurturing spirit, a definite love for God and a love for others.

God has blessed this woman beyond measure. To be a wife, mother, employee, grandmother, minister of the gospel and an author – the sky is the limit and beyond. God bless you, proud to call you my spiritual daughter and congratulations on your second editon.

Lady Cheryl E. Owens
First Lady of New Hope Baptist Church

This book has given me strength, comfort and encouragement. It is easy to read and understand. Not long, but strong. Thank you for allowing God to inspire you to write this book.

Lady Carol Sharp
First Lady of Concord Missionary Baptist Church

"I See You, and I Know!" by Sheila G. Bullock is a phenomenal read! As you read this book of inspiration, prepare to be uplifted with a gentle nudge of love and assurance that God has you on His mind.

Reading this book pulls your inner peace into alignment with the infallible written Word of God. If you have ever felt like God has turned His eyes away from you and your situation, read this book and that feeling will not be invited back into your world. Get ready to rise out of the ashes of uncertainty into the realm of absolute assurance that God Sees You and He most certainly knows!

Rev. James N. Williams, Pastor
Wells Cathedral, COGIC

I would like to take advantage of this wonderful opportunity to express my experiences while reading this extremely inspiring book.

I was drawn into the spirit of which Minister Bullock wrote, so passionately with warmth and gentleness of expression. The compassion in which she showed for the little creatures and her overwhelming love for God and God's people.

I cried, I chuckled and I also praise God! Thank you Minister Sheila Bullock, for letting the Lord use you to touch the hearts and so many lives in such a marvelous way. Our book club was blessed reading your first book.

Looking forward to the pleasure of reading your next book. Congratulations!

Dr. Frances E. Billups Ph.T
Dean of Living Waters Christian Education Center Inc.

"I See You and I Know" is such an inspirational message of hope and restoration. This book will take you on a journey towards God's love and envelop you in His presence assuring us of His peace. This book reminds us we are not alone. The author reminds us through the Psalms that God's All Seeing Eye and Inescapable Presence is always with us no matter the situations we face. Such an encouragement that you want to add this book to your collection.

Minister Sharon D. Maye
First Lady of Calvary Temple UHCA

As I ponder, I want to expound on Chapter 7 of "I See You, and I Know". It's like looking in the mirror. When I totally surrendered all to G-d, there was no clarity for the purpose at that moment, because of me being in a very dark space in my life. A new marriage, the lost of our Father, the lost of my mother-in-love. Incarceration and betrayal among the masses and alcohol and drug addiction had taken its course. Then one day, I was ready to throw in the towel for all was very overwhelming. I could hear our mother say "TC, give it all to G-d and watch and see what He will do!" At that moment I fell on my knees and surrendered 100% of my life to G-d and He fixed all my wounds, worries, circumstances and doubts <u>instantly</u>!

As you wrote in Chapter 7, *"When we give Him complete control, we can give it to Him knowing He will never make a mistake."* Thank you Sister for sharing and blessing my wife and I with this book.

Troy and Tanisha Williams

My dear Sister, your book has been an inspiration to me in a few ways. I am thankful to have a sister that loves people the way you do. As I reflect on the book as well as Psalms 139, it is a constant reminder that God sees everything, He hears everything, and He is everywhere all at the same time. However, we as humans, but even more we as Christians, tend to think that God does not see us when we do things that we are not supposed to do, go places we should not go, and say things we should not say. He is an all-seeing and all-knowing God, but we continue our own way. God is such a loving God and He continues to love us despite our faults and shortcomings. If there was a time to live for Christ, it is now more than ever. The world is in such a reckless state, and I do not know if a person is going to make it without Christ. So, I say to my Sis, Sister-Mom congratulations to you on your book. As I stated earlier, you have inspired me and now I have begun drafting my own book. Stay tuned, I love you to life.

Your brother,
Maurice

While reading this powerful book by "Lady B" (that is what I call her), I'm reminded that for years, I forgot that God sees me and knows everything about me – because He loves and cares for me so much, I realize that it's okay to just be me. For I am fearfully and wonderfully made in His image. Lady B, thank you for the inspiration and for this book.

Your Sister,
Theresa

The emergence and popularity of social media is a clear indication of the need to be seen and heard. The desire to be validated is commonplace and often times drives us to make the decisions we make.

"I See You, and I Know" highlights this need and brings assurance that there is someone who not only sees you but understands ALL that we go through.

It is refreshing to know that the God who created the universe and everything in it, is concerned with me and is able to address me from His vantage point.

This book is beautifully written and will captivate you with its illustrations of God's Love and Intention for our lives.

Lovingly,
Kevin M. Bullock

"I See You and I Know" is a transformative read that offers a refreshing perspective on spirituality, self-growth, and personal empowerment via God's personal concern for you. Bullock's warm and relatable writing style creates a sense of connection, as if she is personally guiding you through your own journey of gaining a deeper perspective of who God is and His intentions for your life.

One of the strengths of this book is her ability to weave together nature and modern-day relevance. She draws upon scriptures, presenting them in a way that is accessible and applicable to our contemporary lives. Whether you are in a place of high faith or low faith, your faith will reach new levels as you read through her own testimony of how God saw her and the desires of her heart.

This is a must-read for anyone seeking to deepen their understanding of God's concern about them. Her wise and compassionate guidance shines through every page, making this book a true gem in the realm of spiritual self-help literature.

Jessica E. Bullock, LCMHC, LCADC, CCS
Life Options Counseling & Consulting Services

Dear Mom,

"I See You, and I Know" has profoundly impacted my perspective on faith. In the pages of this book, the reader is encouraged to trust in God resonates deeply. Life's challenges may appear insurmountable, yet the narrative emphasizes the vastness of God's understanding and strength. It's a comforting reassurance that our problems, though significant, pale in comparison to the greatness of our God.

This book has encouraged me to recalibrate my focus, understanding that no matter how overwhelming our troubles may seem, God's omnipotence surpasses them all. Thank you for instilling in me the wisdom to trust in His plan, even when life's journey seems daunting.

With love,
Mark Antoine Bullock
(Mr. Idea)

"I See You and I Know" is a captivating masterpiece that intertwines with the depths of your soul, tenderly reminding you of the profound truth: you are never truly alone because God is with you.

This book, with its refreshing perspective, is impactful and leaves an imprint on your mind that lingers long after the last page is turned. Thank you for writing this book.

Lovingly,
Shavon M. Bullock

Upon finishing the book "I See You, and I Know," I was sitting on an island looking at the ocean's moving clouds and crashing waves. The sun was shining so bright, and I thought, "I only like cloudy!" you have to read the book to understand that reference. This book is a captivating journey about faith, G-d's voice, and the power of our connectiveness to nature. Through personal anecdotes, moving insights, and spiritual reflections, Bullock weaves a narrative that entertains, enlightens, and empowers.

Its seamless integration of scriptures, spiritual insights, and life lessons sets this book apart. The author skillfully presents the interconnectedness of all things back to G-d. After reading this book, it was clear that hearing and listening to G-d's voice bridges the gap to some of the questions we always ask.

Throughout the book, Bullock emphasizes the importance of cultivating intuition as a practical tool for navigating life's challenges. She provides readers with practical exercises and techniques for honing their intuitive abilities, encouraging them to trust their inner guidance and tap into the wisdom of their higher selves.

However, the message of prayer, connection, and unity truly sets "I See You and I Know" apart from other written texts. It's a great reminder to us all that we should explore and study scriptures daily and how it is important to stay watchful and prayerful to hear G-d's voice clearly. I love you Mom.

Kaveena A.S. Miller, M.A.
Education and Curriculum Specialist
Creator of Coffee & Curriculum©

"I See You and I Know" is a thought-provoking and inspiring read that challenges readers to explore the depths of their relationship with G-d and embrace the beautiful creations He made around us. Mrs. Bullock's words of spiritual wisdom creates a compelling narrative that will leave a lasting impact on anyone seeking to deepen their understanding of themselves and how G-d truly sees us and knows who we are. With love and warmth.

Akeem Miller
International Diplomacy Specialist
U.S. – China Relations Strategist

God has empowered His people to be able to achieve anything their hearts desire. "I See You, and I Know" conveys that if we put God first and have a right relationship with Him, He will bless us.

This was an awesome and phenomenal book, it was intriguing, thought provoking, enlightening, powerful, knowledgeable, and encouraging. It has given me a new perspective as a Christian. It has enabled me to take a serious inventory on my life, asking God where have I fallen short and how can I become a better servant for Him?

"I See YOU and I Know" is a guide to how we're supposed to model ourselves as believers in Christ. We're God's ambassadors and we must live a life pleasing to Him, so that He receives all glory.

Minister Sheila Summers
Biblical Studies, B.A.

In her first book, "I See You, and I Know, Minister Sheila Bullock delved into a very familiar theme for Christians: The overwhelming presence of God in every aspect of the lives of His children. She examined **Psalm 139** and made it abundantly clear that this Divine Presence is and should be a source of comfort, encouragement and joy.

Minister Bullock pointed out that knowing and fully embracing the fact that God's intimate knowledge of us is something that should fill us with exceeding joy, not fear. We can be our authentic selves, knowing that God understands our struggles, knows we are finite creatures, and yet, stands with open arms ready to forgive and accept us as His own. Despite our mistakes, failures, and doubts, God's love is never-ending, and always present.

"I See You, and I Know! is an acknowledgment that whoever we are, whatever our past or present, God's omnipresent spirit is also there; guiding, protecting, forgiving, and loving us on this journey called life. This book is a beautiful and comforting reassurance that no matter what, God's love will never waiver or fail.

Frances Moore, MSW, LCSW, ACSW

Minister Sheila Bullock's first book *"I See You, and I Know!"* expounds on the scripture **Psalm 139** in such a fascinating way that draws the reader in. Her writing style is such that a new *Christian* or a *Seasoned Saint* could glean a refreshing revelation within its pages. The prayers at the end of each chapter helps to draw the reader closer to God and deepens the relationship between the Christian and God by encouraging the reader to read the prayers out loud. *"I See You, and I Know!"* acknowledges God's omniscience and intimate knowledge of the reader and thus transforms their Christian journey.

Minister Bullock's book *"I See You, and I Know!"* acknowledges that God knows every aspect of our being, both externally and internally and Minister Bullock weaves personal anecdotes and stories to reinforce the scripture **Psalm 139.** Minister Bullock helps the reader reflect on the personal and profound nature of God's knowledge and understanding about them as individuals which in turn will help to strengthen their personal relationship with God.

Kimberly P. Moore-Jones, LCSW, ACSW

If you've ever thought of getting away with something and thinking that no one will know about it, think again! In this extremely powerful discourse of Psalm 139, Minister Bullock's (Sheila's) passion for helping all generations, has managed to fill each page with invaluable wisdom and insight. Understanding that God sees us, understands us, and continues to lead us in everything we say and do is encouraging and challenging in order to seek intimacy with God every day. Her beautiful life examples are plain enough, and are examples of what the average person experiences from day to day. Throughout this book, we get a deeper understanding of the loving nature of our Heavenly Father.

Sheila is a fierce lover of God and wants us to know that we are never alone. This book is both a source of comfort for those who honor God and a warning to those who defy Him.

Sister Rubye

The very first thing that grabbed my attention was written below the author's name on the front cover of the book, "You will never be the same after reading Psalm 139. It will change your entire life." Well, I had already read Psalm 139 more than once. However, needless to say, I read it again! When I began reading the book, I was unable to put it down.

I have always known that God is all-seeing and all-knowing but the real-life situations and examples presented by the author were startling reminders of His omnipotence. I have always tried to 'listen' for God's voice. I must admit that I have difficulty hearing it. The author reminded me that God is always communicating with us (me) even though His voice is not always audible. I was also reminded that not everyone worships in the same manner; that God sees my heart and knows my thoughts so my worship doesn't have to be like anyone else's.

The anecdote of the little bird in the middle of the road reminds me that God will always make a way. We just need to trust him. A deacon from my church used to say, "If you pray, don't worry and if you worry, don't pray." I am a 'worrier' and I readily admit it! The author reminded me that God will protect me just as he protected that tiny bird.

I particularly liked the prayers at the end of each chapter of the book. They were spot on! I also liked the author's suggestion to write down scriptures and try to memorize them. Overall, I found the book very encouraging and up-lifting. It should not be read once and put away as I did. It is definitely worth reading over and over again! Kudos to the author!

Madge Stewart

Have you ever felt that God doesn't know you or that you are so insignificant in the eyes of God? Maybe because of where you are, what you lack, and what you might not have been able to accomplish, or even where you were born? Diving into this easy-to-read book will tell you otherwise. Can you reconcile what God's word says in Luke 12:7 that "even the hairs on your head are all numbered?" Then you are in for a treat with Sheila Bullock's book "I See You and I Know" because the God who knows and sees you has your back, and He is ready to lead you if you are ready to give him your hand.

In this book, you are the main character here, Sheila's exposition through Psalms 139 speaks to you directly. You feel God's word speaking over your life as she weaves through the verses with humorous personal stories that will captivate your attention.

Personally, reading this book, I felt the Father inviting me in. Sometimes life can be overwhelming, and we tend to downplay what God's Word says, but journeying through Psalms 139 with Sheila is reassuring and brings one's faith to life, sparking hope and love from a Father who cares – thus He Sees us, and He Knows!

Lady Sheila Bullock has been a friend and an inspirational mentor to me. Meeting her at a mutual friend's women's event several years ago, her exhortation sparked some joy and love in my heart towards her and her ministry. She inspires me to keep loving the Lord and in the capacity of a pastor's wife. I'm blessed and privileged to know her. She is a real blessing to the body of Christ.

Juliana Gardiner, Author of
"Trusting God Beyond Limits"

Sheila Bullock, the spiritual author, uses realistic anecdotes that serve as a gentle reminder: the Lord created me. It is in trusting God's lead that I find my truest path—the one that resonates with purpose and promise.

I am a witness to the Lord's inescapable presence that has saved my life time and time again. My heart is full of hope and excitement as I pray the many prayers prescribed by the author, based on the truth of God's Word.

Serena Farquharson-Torres, Ph.D., Esq.

The power of the spirit runs deep in "I see you and I know" by the talented Sheila Bullock. She writes with grace and empathy as she translates Psalm 139 in a way that accords and relates to modern speech and life. As you transcend on a journey with Sheila through her story, you can feel the power of the Lord and you know that even in our darkest and most dismal hour, the Lord is present. Through our faith in His endless love, we will always walk in light with Him.

Rose Czyzyk

The words in "I See You, and I Know" are precisely what we need for such a time as this. You will walk away covered in a blanket of God's comfort and love – for you are the apple of His eye.

Evelyn Vasquez

For being her first published book, Sheila Bullock will touch your heart with each word she writes. I have reached for Sheila's book many times when grieving the loss of loved ones. I am comforted when I read, "I see you and I know you."

I am so looking forward to her next book!

Nell Bartholomew

"I See YOU, and I Know!" is a beautifully written book about the unwavering presence of God in our lives. In a world where we can easily become overwhelmed by personal struggles and daily responsibilities, the author's words reassure us that God is with us through it all, guiding us on our path and strengthening us for the road ahead. This book offers a welcome reminder that God doesn't always reveal Himself in big, jaw-dropping ways, sometimes God can be found in the sunshine after the rain or the smile of a child or the beauty of a small bird. From beginning to end, this book gives the reader the gift of helping us to slow down and think about all the ways that God is present and speaking to us in our daily lives - if we just take the time to look and listen!

Megan Shull

I See YOU, and I Know! G_d All-Seeing Eyes and Inescapable Presence by Sheila Bullock comforts the soul. It is a thrilling book of encouragement, prayers, scriptures, and songs that feed and nourish your soul. The book allows one to acknowledge and understand that the presence of God is always with you. It gives hope to the brokenhearted, weary, and hopeless individual. The book emphasizes the omnipresent, omnipotent, and omniscient presence of God through His Son, Jesus Christ, and that His spirit is always with you.

What I love about each chapter is that it highlights scriptures and encourages readers to pray out loud. This method awakens one's soul allowing one to access the presence of God.

Sheila reminds us of the incompatible Father, who will never leave us nor forsake us. He is always in control. No matter what situation you find yourself in, God sees and He knows! Additionally, Sheila tries to please God in everything she does. She knows that even with a small voice or shout, God hears her.

Psalms 139 is one of my favorite bible scriptures as it reminds me that God's eyes are always on me and that He knows my rising, and my sitting down.

Sharon Lyn

ACKNOWLEDGMENTS

This book would not been possible without the support of my family and special friends.

To my beloved Mother Eula L. Williams. Thank you for teaching and training me with all your organizational skills. Thank you for showing me how to love my husband through your example and how to be a great mother. I am the woman I am because of you. I love you more than you'll ever know.

To my mother and father-in-love, Trustee Nathaniel Bullock, Sr., and Mother Ruth Bullock, thank you for the many years of encouragement, love, and support that you have given me for more than forty-five years. You both are dear to my heart.

To my sons and daughter-in-loves, Kevin (Jessica), Mark (Shavon) and Kaveena (Akeem). Thank you for believing in me and always allowing me to be in your lives. To my extended family, DeJuan and Alisha Stanley, who I love very much, thank you for your prayers and support; and to a very special young lady, Mrs. Aisha Mgeni-John, thank you for your friendship and encouragement.

To my Prayer Warriors—Evangelist Leona Dawson; Evangelist Willye Daniels; my brother, Pastor James Williams; my sister, Lady Sharon

Maye; my son, Elder Mark Bullock and a good friend, Ms. Renee Copes. Thank you for standing in the gap whenever I called on you for prayer requests.

To my godmother, Mother Gloria Francis, for always keeping me and my family in prayer. Thank you for your encouragement – you have never changed.

To my dear friend Pastor Regina Gainer, whose books have inspired me to follow through in writing my own book.

To Pastor Mildred Williams: Although you came into my life just a few years ago, I thank you for your trailblazing spirit that leads a path for young ladies to follow. You are amazing!

SPECIAL ACKNOWLEDGEMENT

To my husband, friend, and pastor, Nathaniel Bullock Jr. Thank you for always encouraging me to go beyond what I can see. Thank you for your patience and long hours of waiting for me in the car. I honor and appreciate the gift that G-d has given to you to teach the Word in season and out of season. Your teaching has inspired me more than you'll ever know. Keep living the life!

PRECIOUS MEMORIES

To my Daddy, the late Reverend James W. Williams. Thank you for always believing in me, teaching me to pray, training me to love others and to treat people with respect. I miss you deeply.

The late Mother Alberta Barnes (my grandmother) for teaching me to dream.

The late Rita Ellis (my aunt) for passing on her creativity.

The late Bishop Nathan Jackson (my first pastor) for the foundation, instructions, and preaching he taught me growing up from a child to teen and into my young adult years.

A special thank you to my daughter, Mrs. Kaveena A.S. Miller, who gave me the inspiration that started my journey into writing.

TO ALL READERS

Why the "o" is omitted when writing G-d's name.

I have been asked this question time after time when people see any of my writings or if a song sheet is shared with the name "G-d" in the lyrics.

From my research, when religious Jewish newspapers were first printed in pre-Holocaust Europe, many adopted the practice to follow the more stringent opinion and hyphenate the name of G-d, lest at some stage these pages be treated disrespectfully. This practice now extends to all articles, newspapers or magazines printed in Yiddish, English or any other language. However, in sacred texts, the name of G-d is often spelled out in full, since the presumption is that such books will be treated with respect.

I choose to omit the "o" too (emphasis mine).

With love,
Sheila

PROLOGUE

It was a cold winter sunny day in 1999 at approximately seven-thirty in the morning. We started out with our normal routine of getting ready for the day. I had my bags and lunch prepared for my daughter, Kaveena, and me. Kaveena was a bright-eyed four-year-old with her own mind and thoughts.

"I don't like the sun!" she proclaimed.

"You don't like the sun?" I replied.

"No. I only like cloudy!"

You see, the sun was in Kaveena's eyes, and she couldn't see the sky clearly.

We continued our journey to her preschool. I took her inside and followed through signing her in and making sure she was settled in for her day. I gave her a loving hug, and off I went.

As I walked to my car, I looked up and thought about Kaveena's words about the sun. The sky was quite beautiful for that time of the morning, and the clouds seemed to beckon someone to take a look at them. As I opened the door to my car, I looked up at the sky and smiled at the beautiful clouds and heard a Rhema Word in my spirit that said to me, "I see you! and I know!"

For a moment, I stood with my mouth gaping opened because the voice was clear, precise, and without a doubt the voice of G-d[1].

CHAPTER 1

G-D KNOWS YOUR NAME

O L-RD, You have searched me and known me.
—Psalm 139:1

Can you remember a time when someone called your name out loud and you knew he or she wanted your attention? It could have been your parents, a sibling, a friend, an enemy, your boss, children, or your spouse. Depending on the urgency of hearing your name called, how did you respond?

Have you ever experienced G-d calling your name? He is always beckoning us to hear His voice. Sometimes we may hear His voice through prayer, sometimes we may hear His voice while reading His Holy Word, and sometimes the Holy Spirit will gently remind you that G-d is calling you.

One of the definitions for *call*[1] is to communicate. How do you communicate with G-d? Prayer, singing, and praising Him are forms of communication that we can utilize in our daily walk with Him. The

L-RD G-d encourages us with this Scripture in Isaiah 65:24, "It shall come to pass That before they call, I will answer; and while they are still speaking, I will hear."

Our G-d is omniscient. He knows everything! The Scripture tells us in Psalm 90:1–2, "L-RD, You have been our dwelling place in all generations. Before the mountains were brought forth, Or ever You had formed the earth and the world, Even from everlasting to everlasting, You are G-d." You don't have to worry about G-d not knowing you are you. He has already searched you out before you were born. He knew on this day, at this hour, this very minute that you would be reading this book. You see, G-d has plans for you. He has a future for you. He made you in His image, in His likeness, and He loves you. Let me encourage you with this Scripture, Jeremiah 29:11–13: "For I know the thoughts that I think toward you, says the L-RD, thoughts of peace and not of evil, to give you a future and a hope. Then you will call upon Me and go and pray to Me, and I will listen to you. And you will seek Me and find *Me*, when you search for Me with all our heart."

Yes, my friend, *you*! You see, G-d has already searched our hearts and minds, and He knows all about us. He knows your name. Even when we think no one is listening or is concerned, G-d is right there waiting for us. He loves *you* and He is concern about *you*. My husband always says, "G-d wants to reveal more to you than you want to know about Him."

The word *search*[2] means to move around in, go through, or look through in an effort to find something. Another definition for the word *search*[2] is to make a careful examination or investigation. "O L-RD, You have searched me and known me" (Psalms 139:1). No one knows you like G-d does. Only He can see right through you. Only He can see what's in your heart. In the book of Job, chapter 23, verse 10, Job declares, "But

He knows the way that I take; *When* He has tested me, I shall come forth as gold." You see, the Bible tells us in the book of Job that he was an "upright man." Job lost so much, and in this chapter he said he could not find G-d, but he also declared, "He knows the way that I take." Yes, my sister; yes, my brother; G-d has searched us, and He knows all about us. He has made a careful examination of our lives, our ways, our coming in and our going out. He thoroughly knows you and me.

What is in a name? There is a plethora of information on what's in a name. I was a teenager the first time I read the meaning of my name. *Sheila* means "musical" and "unseen faith." The Scripture associated with this meaning is Joshua 1:9: "Have I not commanded you? Be strong and of good courage; do not be afraid, nor be dismayed, for the L-RD your G-d is with you wherever you go." I was very encouraged when I read this, but I didn't know how true this Scripture would come to life until I started getting older and learned how to truly walk with G-d.

I will never forget the times our church had anointing worship services. I always admired saints in the church who could praise G-d loudly. I wanted to have a loud sound too. It didn't happen for me, but I figured maybe when I get a little older, I would have a loud praise. No! Instead, a small whisper would escape with heart-wrenching praise down on the inside. Why couldn't I have a loud praise? I felt as though I was disappointing G-d because He wouldn't be able to really hear me. Have you ever felt as if G-d doesn't hear you? I used to feel that way. Well, during this particular worship service, one of our missionaries was facilitating the worship service with praise, admiration, prophecy, and interpretation of prophecy. When we had this type of service, *no one moved!* There was a fear of reverence in the house of G-d that you could not explain. One thing for sure, G-d was moving by His Spirit. I was standing with my hands lifted and head bowed, praising G-d in my whispering voice. The missionary called my name out and said to me, "Sister Sheila! G-d said for you to continue doing exactly what you are doing. He hears you, and He is pleased." I began to sob. He really did hear me! From that time until now, I realize that G-d hears you even if your praise is not loud. He wants us to worship Him with a true and pure heart. Matthew 5:8 says, "Blessed *are* the pure in heart, for they shall see G-d." From that point on, I was so excited to praise the L-RD that I couldn't wait for the next service and my prayer time.

LET'S GO DEEPER!

Have you ever experienced G-d calling your name? Yes ☐ / No ☐

If your answer is Yes, write about it:

_____
_____
_____
_____

If you answer is No, how do you know?

_____
_____
_____
_____

How do you communicate with G-d?

_____
_____
_____
_____

In Genesis, Chapter 16 – we read the story of Hagar and Ishmael. Hagar was an Egyptian maidservant and was acquired by Sarai when she moved from Canaan to Egypt. She was obligated to do what Sarai asked. Sarai was barren and she gave Hagar to her husband to receive a child. After Hagar announced that she was with child, Sarai mistreated her to the point that Hagar ran away.

In Hagar's despair throughout her ordeal, I can only imagine the humiliation she experienced. The emotional and physical toil that it took on her and the feeling of being alone but, in Genesis 16:7-10 and 13 the scripture reads,

> *"Now the Angel of the L-RD found her by a spring of water in the wilderness, by the spring on the way to Shur. And He said, Hagar, Sarai's maid, where have you come from, and where are you going?"*
>
> *She said, "I am fleeing from the presence of my mistress Sarai." The Angel of the L-RD said to her, "Return to your mistress, and submit yourself under her hand." Then the Angel of the L-RD said to her, "I will multiply your descendants exceedingly, so that they shall not be counted for multitude."*
>
> *Then she called the name of the L-RD who spoke to her, You-Are-the-G-d-who-Sees; for she said, "Have I also here seen Him who sees me?" Therefore, the well was called Be'er La.hai, Roi;"* "EL ROI" THE G-D WHO SEES ME *(emphasis mine)*

How often have you asked yourself these questions?

- I wonder if G-d really knows how I feel. What do you want to say to Him?

_____
_____
_____
_____

- I wonder if G-d knows what I'm going through right now. Tell Him here.

_____
_____
_____
_____

- Does G-d really hear me? Share your thoughts with Him.

_____
_____
_____
_____

The answer to these questions are a resounding "YES", "YES" and "YES".

The Bible have several scriptures to assure us that G-d sees, knows and cares for us. Here are a few scriptures for you to meditate on.

- Joshua 1:9 – *(write out verse)*

  _____
  _____
  _____
  _____

- Isaiah 41:10 – *(write out verse)*

  _____
  _____
  _____
  _____

- Matthew 18:20 – *(write out verse)*

  _____
  _____
  _____
  _____

POINTS TO REMEMBER:
- Our G-d is Omniscient – HE KNOWS EVERYTHING!
- Our G-d is Omnipresent – HE IS EVERYWHERE AT THE SAME TIME!
- Our G-d is Omnipotent – HE IS ALMIGHTY!

One would think reading these scriptures would be enough but sometimes we don't pay attention until we hit a crisis and then "look for G-d" in our desperation.

This is a very familiar scripture that is TRUE FOR US ALL! (Please write it out).

Jeremiah 29:11-13:

_____

_____

_____

_____

_____

_____

_____

_____

What is your Name? _____

Do you know the meaning of your Name? Yes ☐ / No ☐
If yes, write it down. If not, look it up.

_____

_____

Is there a Scripture associated with your Name? Yes ☐ / No ☐
If yes, write down. If not, pray and ask G-d which scripture best fits you.

_____

_____

I love watching The Bionic Woman. I know it's not real but it's funny when she moves her hair away from her ear to listen from a far distance.

We serve a G-d that can hear our voice without us opening our mouths. That's for REAL! The essence of Psalm 139 is that G-D KNOWS AND HEARS ALL THINGS ABOUT YOU!

- When we hurt, we want someone to soothe us; LET HIM COMFORT YOU.
- When we cry, we want someone to dry our tears; HE SEES YOUR TEARS.
- When we laugh, we want someone to celebrate with; HE'S OUR JOY!

Let me encourage you. Write your own prayer to your Heavenly Father.

_____

_____

_____

_____

_____

_____

_____

_____

_____

_____

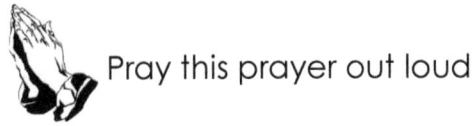 Pray this prayer out loud

Dear Heavenly Father,

I'm so glad You know my name. Even before I was born, You knew me. Please forgive me for not answering You when You call my name. Give me spiritual ears to hear the sound of Your voice in my spirit. You said in Your Word in Isaiah 65:24 (NLT) "I will answer them before they even call to me. While they are still talking about their needs, I will answer their prayers!"

Dear Heavenly Father, when You call me, I will answer. Help me to be obedient to Your Word. Thank you for hearing my prayer.

In Jesus' Name – Amen.

CHAPTER 2

G-D KNOWS WHERE YOU SIT

> *You know my sitting down*
> —Psalm 139:2

Have you ever noticed birds sitting on a wire as you drive down the freeway or sit at the traffic light? Have you ever wondered what they could be thinking? Why do they sit on the wire? Sometimes I think they like to see all the different colored vehicles that zoom by second after second and minute after minute. Or maybe after their morning flight, they need to rest, so they sit above and watch us below. It is said that the birds sit on the wire to stay warm. That is an interesting thought. You see, birds have families, they have fun, they sleep, eat, get sick, hurt, get well, and then they die. Yet they don't worry. We read in Matthew 6:26 (AB), "Look at the birds of the air; they neither sow nor reap nor gather into barns, and yet your heavenly Father keeps feeding them. Are you not worth much more than they?"

I love birds. Let me share another real-life story that happened to me on a sunny Saturday in June 2009. It was approximately twelve-thirty in the afternoon. I worked a half-day to finish up a project I was working on at my place of employment. I had an eye doctor's appointment near my home and proceeded to go my usual way home. As I approached the end of the road that continued around a curve, my eyes darted to the middle of the road. As I continued to drive, I said out loud, "Was that a bird?"

I felt compelled to turn around, and without hesitation, I proceeded back to the road before the curve. Sure enough a beautiful, small, light-brown bird was sitting in the middle of the road.

I asked myself, "Why is she in the middle of the road?" It was as if time stood still. This bird was panting in intervals opening and closing her mouth. She didn't move as the cars were speeding by her. She kept panting. I got out of my car, leaving the door open. I placed my left hand up to stop the oncoming traffic and proceeded to pick up the bird, but for a second, I thought it would be better not to use my bare hands. I had a craft pattern on my car seat that I purchased the day before. I took the pattern envelope and proceeded carefully and cautiously scooping the bird on top of the envelope. As I scooped her on top of the envelope, I began to speak to her in a whisper. I said, "What are you doing here? C'mon, little birdie, I won't hurt you." She didn't try to fly away, so I thought she was probably hurt. I walked slowly across the street onto the sidewalk and placed her on the beautiful green grass next to a large tree. She was still panting. As I returned to my car, parked in the middle of that busy curve in the street, I noticed a line of cars waiting. I waved my hand to indicate "thank you," got back into my car, and turned around to go to my appointment. Not one time during this experience did I hear a car horn blow.

The word *sit*[1] means to rest the body on a supporting surface. It also means to be situated, to be agreeable; to suppress or postpone an action; a period spent sitting.

I don't know how long this bird was sitting in the middle of the road, but G-d knew, and He protected this bird.

Where are you sitting? Are you in the middle of a road? You may be going through a tough time right now. Maybe you're sitting because of a health issue or a marriage hanging on by threads. Maybe you have been looking for a job and everywhere you turn, you don't qualify. Or maybe you feel like no one cares and no one sees what you are going through. Well, let me encourage you that even when things are not going as expected, G-d sees and He knows. Even when you can't voice your opinions or express your views, G-d sees and He knows. Even when your family and friends pass you by, G-d sees and He knows. When you worked so hard for the promotion you finally received, but your colleagues disassociate themselves from you because you don't have a degree, even in this, my friend, He sees and He knows. And because G-d knows, He will open a door for you, make a way for you because He loves you, and has given you destiny and purpose.

G-d will place people in your life that can show you a way out, or give you suggestions or directions that will place your feet in the direction that G-d wants you to go. Let me return to the little bird in the middle of the road.

I drove into the driveway of the establishment to turn around. I looked over to where I left the little bird. She just sat there. For some reason, I just could not leave her. I felt obligated to make sure she was okay. I called the animal hospital, and a young lady answered. I explained to the young lady that I found a bird panting in the middle of the street and that I was able to place her on safe ground. The young lady told me that they don't deal with wildlife. She gave me a number to another animal hospital that may handle this. When I called the next animal hospital, the person on the line told me the same thing, but did suggest that I contact the city's wildlife hotline. I contacted the nearest wildlife hotline. After three rings, I disconnected my call and thought this was silly. By that time, I was late for my appointment. I call my doctor's office and asked them if I could still come in. Yes, the young lady said to me. Sitting and waiting, watching this bird, I still could not drive away, so I called the wildlife hotline again. I let the telephone ring this time, hoping for a person to pick up. Instead, an answering machine voice message began to play. Here is what the message said:

> You have reached the wildlife hotline. If you are calling about an injured bird, please do not attempt to feed it or give it water. Instead, place the injured bird in a box and leave it in a shaded area. Leave your name and number and someone will get back to you.

How ironic is this! I left my name and number and a short message. I said to myself, "I don't have a box!" I looked around in the back seat of my car. What do you think I saw? A small tissue box with one tissue left inside. I took the box, exited the car, and slowly walked over to the bird. She wasn't panting by this time, but her eyes were closed.

Sometimes we don't understand why things happen the way that they do. The song lyrics come to mind, "His eye is on the sparrow, and I know, He watches over me."[2] You see, G-d *knows* where we sit. In each season of our lives, whatever day, week, month, or year you read this book, He knows where you are sitting. He knows your location and where you are situated. He knows when you are inactive and refuse to participate in the game of life. He knows when you are in a comfortable situation and an uncomfortable situation. He knows when you take action and when you don't take action. He knows which way the wind will blow you. He knows your occupation. He knows what you are entitled to. He knows what type of clothing you should be wearing. He knows what looks good on you. Sometimes it fits, and sometimes it doesn't. He knows when you need comforting, and He knows that there may come a day when someone else will have to look after you. He knows when we are financially well established and at our lowest point waiting for funds. He knows when we are patient and when we are impatient. He knows when we make our own opinions and stand firmly for the task. He knows when we let our guards down and don't pay attention. He knows when we fall in love and out of love. He knows when people love us for what we have and don't have. He knows when people use us, abuse us, talk about us, hate us, and take advantage of us. He knows when you are about to face the storm of life, and He prepares people whom you will meet strategically on the road to your destiny and purpose. Finally, and above all, He knows when we **stay in touch** (sit) with Him.

When we sit with G-d, He will continually comfort our hearts. He is the maker of our hearts. He knows how to fix our hearts. He knows how to heal our hearts. Your heart cannot be healed if you don't stay in touch with Him. I can still hear the words from pastors and mothers of the church, "It's a daily walk." To stay in touch with G-d, we must speak with Him often, every day. Our thoughts should speak with Him at all times. You may ask, "Why should I constantly sit with Him if He already knows what I'm going to say or what I'm going to do?" Good question. G-d is everlasting *pure, holy,* and *altogether lovely*! We should seek to be just like Him at all times.

Isaiah 55:6–7 says, "Seek the L-RD while He may be found, Call upon Him while He is near. Let the wicked forsake his way, And the unrighteous man his thoughts; Let him return to the L-RD, And He will have mercy on him; And to our G-d, For He will abundantly pardon." G-d can take care of you at all times. The Scripture tells us in Philippians 4:19, "And my G-d shall supply all your need according to His riches in glory by Christ Jesus."

LET'S GO DEEPER!

I started the chapter by discussing birds and how they sit on the wires. How they have families and yet they don't worry. We read in Matthew 6:26 *"Look at the birds of the air; they neither sow nor reap nor gather into barns, and yet your heavenly Father keeps feeding them. Are you not worth much more than they?"*

I am intentionally repeating some of the same content on purpose. Let's reflect for a moment about this.

Sit[1] – to rest the body on a supporting surface. To be situated. To suppress or postpone an action. A period of time spent sitting.

As I stated earlier, I do not know how long that bird was in the middle of the road, but I do know this. G-d protected this bird!

This bird did not move. This bird kept her eyes close and just kept panting.

You may be going through a tough time right now.

You may need answers and have difficulty waiting for G-d to answer.

Even when we run out of words to say to G-d, He still knows.

The fascinating part about this entire situation is that for me "time stood still" like a movie. I am amazed that the church we now fellowship with is directly around the corner from where I saved this little sparrow.

I was allowed to pick this bird up and carry it across the street and placed her on the grass under a tree. All along while I had her in my hands she was panting with her eyes closed.

What was this bird thinking? As the bird's little chest pounded faster and faster, I gently spoke to her. I don't know how long it was before I kept pausing to leave that area, but I waited because I wanted to see what would happen to her.

She didn't budge. She kept sitting and panting.

We don't understand why things happen the way they do but you best believe, He knows where you sit and when you "sit" (staying in touch) with Him.

- When we sit with G-d, He will continually comfort our hearts.
- He will guide our steps;
- He will give us insights into things that we had no knowledge of;

> Isaiah 55:6-7 invites us to *"Seek ye the L-RD while He may be found, call upon Him while He is near. Let the wicked forsake his way, and the unrighteous man his thoughts: and let him return to the L-RD, and He will have mercy upon him; and to our G-d, for He will abundantly pardon."*

G-d can take care of you at all times. I will leave you with this scripture verse.

> Philippians 4:19 – *"And my G-d shall supply all your need according to His riches in glory by Christ Jesus."*

Let's trust Him more with our lives and everything that concerns us and our families. Seek Him and watch! He will answer you back. Wait patiently for Him and He will guide your steps.

G-d knows all these things, and Psalm 139 speaks about them.

Hearing the L-RD speak into my spirit that "He Sees and Knows" allowed me to take another look inside of "me" - my heart and my life. Knowing that we can never escape from G-d's presence should make you take another self-inventory. Go deeper!

What does that mean? We tend to hide ourselves from ourselves.

We have flaws and scars on the outside that people can see, and we have flaws and scars on the inside that G-d can see.

I was reading an article on health and the body. There was a diagram displayed showing different parts of the organs that were diseased. I immediately thought "WOW" we are intricately put together by G-d. Organs, tissues, bones, muscle. Doctors and Scientists continue to study and seek answers for all the many parts of the human body that house all G-d has placed in us. I believe that is why we have "Specialists". Hundreds of doctors focusing on their "specialty" parts of the body and how our system work.

Our G-d specializes in all of them all at once. He made us and knows us.

Acts 17:28 says, *"For in Him we live and move and have our being."*

Here are three (3) points I want to share with you:

- **Don't give up!** We are living in a time where people are giving up hope. Psalms 42:5 *"Why are thou cast down, O my soul? And why art thou disquieted in me? Hope thou in G-d: for I shall yet praise him for the help of his countenance;* Psalm 46:1 *"G-d is our refuge and strength, a very present help in trouble."*
- **Do the right thing!** Romans 12:17b reminds us *"Be careful to do what is right in the eyes of everyone."* These are times when we

have to take serious inventory of our lives and our relationship with G-d; and,

- **Listen for the Voice of G-d!** Isaiah 65:24 reads *"It shall come to pass that before they call, I will answer; and while they are still speaking, I will hear."* My husband always say, "G-d has more to say to us, than we have to say to Him." I encourage you to spend more time with Jesus through prayer, reading and meditating on His Holy Word.

We live in a very fast, busy world. Since the pandemic hit, it has slowed most of us down to the point where we have no choice but to get quiet and still. Stop, pay attention and find out what G-d is saying to you. He does "See you and He definitely Knows!

Let me encourage you to write your own prayer as you **sit** (stay in touch) with your Heavenly Father in your quiet time.

_____

_____

_____

_____

_____

_____

_____

_____

_____

_____

_____

_____

_____

_____

_____

_____

_____

_____

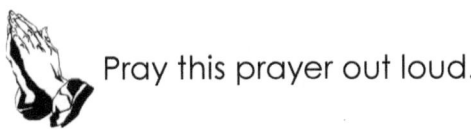 Pray this prayer out loud.

Dear Heavenly Father,

Thank You for noticing when I sit in the arena of life. Please help me to trust You daily as I continue this journey. Please forgive me when I am impatient and not loving as I should be. I want to seek Your face always. Help me to stay in touch (sit) with You at all times and in every circumstance I go through.

Thank You for hearing my prayer.
In Jesus' Name - Amen.

CHAPTER 3

G-D KNOWS WHEN YOU RISE

You know my sitting down and my rising up.
—Psalm 139:2

To everything there is a season, and a time for every matter *or* purpose under heaven: A time to be born and a time to die, a time to plant and a time to pluck up what is planted, A time to kill and a time to heal, a time to break down and a time to build up, A time to weep and a time to laugh, a time to mourn and a time to dance, A time to cast away stones and a time to gather stones together, a time to embrace and a time to refrain from embracing, A time to get and a time to lose, a time to keep and a time to cast away, A time to rend and a time to sew, a time to keep silence and a time to speak, A time to love and a time to hate, a time for war and a time for peace.—Ecclesiastes 3:1–8 (AB)

There is a time when we must rise up and look to Jesus, who is the author and finisher of our faith. (Read Hebrews 12:2).

To rise[1] means to get up from a sitting position or get up after falling or being thrown down. There is a song inspired and written from Psalm 68:1. You may have heard it sung. "Let G-d arise and my enemies be scattered!" What does that mean? G-d allows us to rise above the occasions in our lives. We become active again. We rise above the visible horizon by approaching the situation with faith. We become elevated and increase in rank. We gain influence and power over our situations. We become originators instead of followers. Only with G-d can we begin to produce, advance, and succeed. As it is written in Isaiah 40:31 (KJV), "But they that wait upon the L-RD shall renew their strength; they shall mount up with wings as eagles; they shall run, and not be weary; and they shall walk, and not faint."

Let me continue with my story. I began this chapter with the verse from Ecclesiastes 3:1-8. Well, it was time for me to continue speaking to this bird. As I approached her, I said, "Hi birdie, hello." I will never forget this bird's eyes. Looking at her, I realized that she wasn't so little. She was a medium-sized bird, and she was beautiful. She opened her eyes and moved her head slightly as if to say, "Who are you?" She looked up at me. I spoke to her, "C'mon, let's get you into this box. As I proceeded to scoop her inside the box, what do you think happened? Yes! She flew up and across the way onto a tree branch. I was so shocked and happy at the same time. I tried to wait around to see if she would fly to the next branch. It was very warm that day, and I thought she might be thirsty. I had an unopened bottle of water in the car. I retrieved the bottle of water and looked for a small trench in the driveway near where she was perched. I poured out the entire bottle of water in the trench just in case she was thirsty, and I proceeded to my appointment.

This word *rise*[1] also means to move from a lower to a higher position. When you are down, He can raise you up. We can move from a lower to a higher position or place in our lives. We can increase in height. We can stand up straight and tall. Our reputations can grow with good status. We can increase in strength, just like this little bird in the middle of the road. This bird was able to rise up and fly to an even better place. As the L-RD Jesus says in Matthew 6:26, "Look at the birds of the air, for they neither sow nor reap nor gather into barns; yet your heavenly Father feeds them. Are you not of more value than they?" We can become valuable and allow G-d to resurrect us again. "Revive us, L-RD!" We can rise to the occasion and look forward to starting over again and again. How can I be so sure? Matthew 6:33 says, "But seek first the kingdom of G-d and His righteousness, and all these things shall be added to you." Only because of His grace and mercy can we rise up out of dire situations. We can rise up and be the men and women that G-d is looking for in these last days. In Lamentations 3:22–24, we read, *Through* the L-RD's mercies we are not consumed, Because His compassions fail not. *They are* new every morning; Great *is* Your faithfulness. "The L-RD is my portion," says my soul, "Therefore I hope in Him!"

You see, my friend, we cannot escape G-d's all-seeing eye. Yes, He loves us, and He cares for us. No matter what situation you find yourself in at this very moment, sitting or rising, G-d sees and He knows!

LET'S GO DEEPER!

In the book of Luke 13:10-13 (NIV), we read about a woman who was bent over for 18 years.

Luke 13:10-13 (NIV)
[10] On a Sabbath Jesus was teaching in one of the synagogues, [11] and a woman was there who had been crippled by a spirit for eighteen years. She was bent over and could not straighten up at all. [12] When Jesus saw her, he called her forward and said to her, "Woman, you are set free from your infirmity." [13] Then he put his hands on her, and immediately she straightened up and praised God.

The amazing thought about this woman is that she did not let her infirmity keep her from people. She ventured out to the synagogue. No doubt she was past the embarrassment of being in the condition she was in.

How often have we not felt well only to stay home from service. I remember on several occasions where I had a complete migraine headache but ventured out to service because (1), I had a position to fulfill and (2), I didn't want to miss service. This was a time when there were no "online" services. I believe G-d honored my commitment to Him.

Imagine this woman went to service as she had done many times before but this time, her life would change forever.

Let's take a closer look at the rise of this young lady.

Verse 12 – *"And when Jesus **saw her, he called her to him**……*

Don't think that Jesus doesn't see us when we make sacrifices or when we are downtrodden. Was there ever a time that Jesus came to your rescue? When? Write it down.

_____

_____

_____

_____

_____

_____

Verse 12 continues – *"and **said unto her, Woman, thou art loosed from thine infirmity**……*

What a phenomenal sentence. Jesus spoke directly to her. He is speaking to us today but if we are not "in place", if we are too busy to take time out to hear His voice, we will miss Him every time.

Why do you think G-d wants to speak to you?

_____

_____

_____

_____

_____

_____

There are so many precious promises that He wants to share with you through His Word. He's always speaking but we must take time (quiet time) to listen. Be consistent in your quiet time and He will speak to you.

Verse 13 – *"And **he laid his hands on her**: and **immediately she was made straight, and glorified G-d.**"*

The touch of G-d through the Holy Spirit still touches men and women, boys and girls today through prayer and His Word. We must continue to seek His face.

Sometimes, before we can rise up out of our situations, we have to have a mindset that it won't always be this way. That is where "HOPE" comes into play.

Psalm 42:11 (KJV)
Why art thou cast down, O my soul? And why are thou disquieted within me? **Hope thou in G-d**; *For I shall yet praise him, who is the health of my countenance, and my G-d."* (emphasis mine)

Just like this woman who suffered for many years was raised up out of her condition, we can have hope to rise out of our situations. G-d Sees exactly what you are going through. He sees exactly where you are, when it happened, why it happened and He wants to heal you, comfort you and give you a hope and a future.

Let me encourage you.

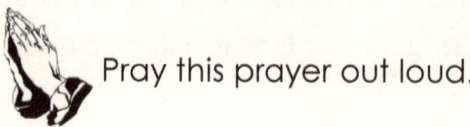 Pray this prayer out loud.

Dear Heavenly Father,

Thank You for the days when we rise above life situations. Thank You for strengthening us and renewing us daily. As it is written in Your Word in Psalm 63:1–5, "O G-d, You are my G-d; Early will I seek You; My soul thirsts for You; My flesh longs for You in a dry and thirsty land where there is no water. So I have looked for You in the sanctuary, To see Your power and Your glory. Because Your lovingkindness is better than life, my lips shall praise You. Thus I will bless You while I live; I will lift up my hands in Your name. My soul shall be satisfied as with marrow and fatness, and my mouth shall praise You with joyful lips." Help us always to be mindful of these times in our lives when You allow us to rise above our circumstances and situations. We look to You Father G-d and praise Your Holy name.

In Jesus' Name – Amen.

CHAPTER 4

G-D UNDERSTANDS YOUR THOUGHTS

You understand my thought afar off.
—Psalm 139:2

Have you ever wondered what G-d is thinking? Have you ever wondered what He thinks when you do something good? When you do something bad? Have you ever sat down and thought, *What is G-d thinking about?* Let's pause and think about that for a moment. Sometimes, I feel like I am the only person G-d is focused on when I think of Him. I feel like it's just me and Him. In the gospel according to John 8:29, Jesus told His disciples, "And He who sent Me is with Me. The Father has not left Me alone, for I always do those things that please Him." How awesome is this statement from our L-RD and Savior? What are your thoughts about this Scripture? Reading this Scripture immediately encouraged me to think, *What can I do to please our heavenly Father?* In every area of our lives, there are thoughts. When we have the mind of Christ, we can have good thoughts. Yes, G-d understands our thoughts from afar. Afar? Yes! The word *afar*[1] means from, at, or to a distance; far away. Before you can think, He already knows what you are thinking. Have you ever experienced knowing when someone was going to say something to you *before* they opened his or her mouth? I have. Most of the time, I know beforehand when my husband will speak. I turn to him and say, "Yes? You are going to say something?" He always shakes his head and replies, "How did you know I was going to say something?" Now hold on! I cannot read his thoughts, nor do I want to; but I have been with him for so many years that I have studied his movements, his voice, breathing patterns, and so forth. He is my husband! You should know something about the person you married. Well, what do you expect from our heavenly Father? *He made you!* We read in Isaiah 46:10, Declaring the end from the beginning, And from ancient times *things* that are not *yet* done, saying, 'My counsel shall stand, And I will do all My pleasure.' Let me ask you a question. "Are you shaking your head as I am?" Just like the little bird in the middle of the road, G-d knew from afar that I would be traveling that road going to the doctor's office. G-d also knew that I would stop to rescue the bird.

Yes, my dear friend, He knows your thoughts from afar. Philippians 4:8 is an excellent passage to memorize and rehearse often to train your mind. "Finally brethren, whatsoever things are true, whatsoever things are honest, whatsoever things are just, whatsoever things are pure, whatsoever things are lovely, whatsoever things are of good report; if there be any virtue, and if there be any praise, think on these things."

There are fifty-four passages of Scripture that you can read and meditate on for a healthy thought life. I will not list all fifty-four passages, but here is a short list of my favorite ones.

*Psalm 63:6 (ESV): "When I remember you upon my bed, and meditate on you in the watches of the night."

*Psalm 104:34 (ESV): "May my meditation be pleasing to him, for I rejoice in the L-RD."

*Psalm 119:11 (ESV): "I have stored up your word in my heart, that I might not sin against you."

*Psalm 119:15 (ESV): "I will meditate on your precepts and fix my eyes on your ways."

*Psalm 119:55 (ESV): "I remember your name in the night, O L-RD, and keep your law."

*Psalm 119:97 (ESV): "Oh how I love your law! It is my meditation all the day."

*Psalm 119:148 (ESV): "My eyes are awake before the watches of the night, that I may meditate on your promise."

*Psalm 143:5 (ESV): "I remember the days of old; I meditate on all that you have done; I ponder the work of your hands."

*Isaiah 26:3 (ESV): "You keep him in perfect peace whose mind is stayed on you, because he trusts in you."

*John 10:27–30 (ESV): "My sheep hear my voice, and I know them, and they follow me. I give them eternal life, and they will never perish, and no one will snatch them out of my hand. My Father, who has given them to me, is greater than all, and no one is able to snatch them out of the Father's hand. I and the Father are one."

I encourage you to pray, seek the L-RD, and mediate on His Word. It helps to write the Scriptures in your notepad on your electronic device or use the old-fashioned method and write them on small index cards. Place them in your purse or tote bag and refer to them often. You can share with a friend, or encourage someone who may be having a rough day. You don't know what assignment the L-RD may give you, so be prepared.

I am reminded of the commandments that G-d gave Moses to relay to Israel. After he told them of the commandments and statues that the L-RD commanded, he then gave these instructions in Deuteronomy 6:6–9: "And these words which I command you today shall be in your heart. You shall teach them diligently to your children, and shall talk of them when you sit in your house, when you walk by the way, when you lie down, and when you rise up. You shall bind them as a sign on your hand, and they shall be as frontlets between your eyes. You shall write them on the doorposts of your house and on your gates."

The commandments from G-d were so important that Moses directed the nation to do everything possible to remember them and to incorporate them into everyday life.

What about us today? The Word of G-d has not changed, nor will it change. This is a great lesson for us to live by and to teach our children. We can share with them when we have family meetings, while riding in the car, cleaning the house, or even have a Scripture recitation contest. When you meditate on the Word of G-d, you will change for the better and can help someone else. Feed your mind today!

LET'S GO DEEPER!

Thought[2] - the capacity or faculty of thinking, reasoning, imagining, etc.

Think[3] - to have a conscious mind, to some extent of reasoning, remembering experiences, making rational decisions, etc.

Have you ever sat down to think what G-d may be thinking about? What are your thoughts?

_____

_____

_____

_____

_____

_____

_____

John 8:29
"And He who sent Me is with me. The Father has not left me alone, for I always do those things that please Him."

What are your thoughts about this scripture?
- If the L-RD Jesus always did those things that pleased the Father, what about us?

Afar – means to a distance – far away.
Before we can think, G-d already knows what you are thinking.

G-d knew from afar that I would be traveling that road going to the doctor and knew that I would stop to rescue that bird.

He knows our ways, our attitudes, our perceptions of one another. We don't even have to open our mouths because he can read our minds but we have the wonderful task to "retrain" our minds.

Philippians 4:8 encourages us to "think on things" that are:
- True, honest, just, pure, lovely and those things that are of a good report.
- ONLY, if there be any virtue and praise, then we ought to "think" on those things. (emphasis added)

Search the scriptures for yourself. You will find many passages that will help you have a healthy "thought life".

Here is an encouraging scripture to mediate on.

Joshua 1:8 (NKJV)
This Book of the Law shall not depart from your mouth, but you shall meditate in it day and night, that you may observe to do according to all that is written in it. For then you will make your way prosperous, and then you will have good success.

Write a few passages that you found:

G-d gave Moses a commandment to relay to the Israelites and this still holds true for us. Deuteronomy 6:6-9. I like to refer to it often.

Deuteronomy 6:6-9 (NIV)
These commandments that I give you today are to be on your hearts. Impress them on your children. Talk about them when you sit at home and when you walk along the road, when you lie down and when you get up. Tie them as symbols on your hands and bind them on your foreheads. Write them on the doorframes of your houses and on your gates.

If you haven't started, today I invite you to meditate on G-d's Holy Word; meditate on Him; mediate on His goodness and seek His Face daily in every area of your life. Share your thoughts, He already knows.

_____

_____

_____

_____

_____

_____

_____

_____

_____

Let me encourage you.

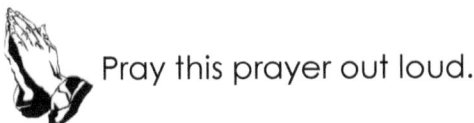 Pray this prayer out loud.

Dear Heavenly Father,

We come to You with a humble spirit. Please help us to meditate on Your Holy Word so that we may have healthy thought lives. We want to be pleasing in Your sight. We want to have the mind of Your dear Son, the L-RD Jesus. As the Scripture says in Philippians 4:8, we want to think on things that are true, things that are honest, things that are just, things that are pure, things that are lovely, things that will be pleasing in Your sight. We look to You and You alone to accomplish this. Thank You for hearing our prayer.

In Jesus' Name – Amen.

CHAPTER 5

G-D HANDS ARE UPON ME!

You have beset me behind and before,
And laid Your hand upon me.
Such knowledge is too wonderful for me;
It is high, I cannot attain it.
—Psalm 139:5–6

Have you ever been in a very tight space? Not much room in front of you, very little behind you, and the sides almost touching you? That was my experience when I had an MRI. It's even more frightening when you are claustrophobic. Now there are open MRI machines to make these tests more tolerable. The word *beset*[1] means to surround from all sides. How exciting to know that G-d's hands are upon me and that He has me surrounded by His love, His presence, and His all-seeing eye!

My husband and I experienced G-d's hands upon us particularly on March 7, 2014.

It was on a Friday evening, and we were coming home from a powerful prayer service. As we sat at the traffic light waiting for it to turn green, I was sharing with my husband how the power of G-d moved mightily in the prayer. Suddenly, we saw an oncoming car drive directly toward us with no sign of stopping. There were no headlights, and I said to my husband, "Honey, is that car coming directly toward us? He doesn't have any headlights." I cried out, "He's gonna hit us! Jesus! Jesus! Jesus!" When the airbags deployed, I kept saying, "Jesus, Jesus, Jesus!" I couldn't say anything else.

The incident took us on a journey that I will never forget. Days and weeks afterwards, I found myself sitting, not being able to do much of anything, but I remember one day looking up toward heaven and saying to the L-RD, "I know You see." Every day the L-RD wakes me up, I thank Him for sparing my life and allowing me to see another day. G-d's hand was upon us that night.

Remember the Scripture from Job:23:10? "But He knows the way that I take; When He has tested me, I shall come forth as gold." A couple of months after the accident, I had a doctor's appointment, and while I was waiting, I glanced over the brochures that were sitting on a table. One of the brochures was information on knee replacement. You see, my Dad needed knee surgery but kept putting it off. I read the free brochure and took one to give to my Dad. After he reviewed it, he decided to speak with his doctor. *G-d knows where we sit!* When my Dad went for pretesting for his knee, one of the test came back negative for his heart. Within weeks, my dad had open-heart surgery to replace one of his valves. We know it was only by the grace of G-d that our Dad was able to have this surgery. G-d not only cares about you and your well-being, but your loved ones and those who surround you.

"*Such* knowledge is too wonderful for me; It is high, I cannot attain it" (Psalm 139:6). When I think about this verse, it makes me shout, "Hallelujah!" The Word of G-d says in Isaiah 55:8–9, "For My thoughts *are* not your thoughts, Nor *are* your ways My ways," says the L-RD. "For as the heavens are higher than the earth, So are My ways higher than your ways, And My thoughts than your thoughts." Sometimes we don't understand why things happen the way they do. We try to comprehend, we shake our heads, point our fingers and blame others and ourselves. But G-d has His eye on us, and we are in His Hands.

In Matthew 6:25, our L-RD Jesus said to His disciples, "Therefore I say to you, do not worry about your life, what you will eat or what you will drink; nor about your body, what you will put on. Is not life more than food and the body more than clothing?" G-d wants us to trust Him in all things. Even when we need to make important decisions, He will guide us. Proverbs 3:5–8 says, "Trust in the L-RD with all your heart, And lean not on your own understanding; In all your ways acknowledge Him, And He shall direct your paths. Do not be wise in your own eyes; Fear the L-RD and depart from evil. It will be health to your flesh, And strength to your bones."

What about the little bird that was in the middle of the road? Well, let me conclude the story.

When I arrived at the doctor's office, I had to wait a little longer because I arrived past my appointment. I wasn't upset about the wait. I couldn't stop thinking about the little bird that I was able to rescue. As I sat waiting to be called, my cell phone starting ringing. Guess who? It was the wildlife center. I could not believe that I received a call back on a Saturday afternoon. The gentleman on the line asked me if I was the person who called about the injured bird. I replied, "yes." I went on to explain to him what had happened. He told me that the bird was very lucky. I asked the gentleman why the bird was panting. He replied that the bird was probably flying too low and most likely got nipped by a car, which disoriented the bird, so she landed in the middle of the road. The bird was panting because she was scared and didn't know what had happened.

Nipped? I wondered. I couldn't get that out of my mind. As I looked at the definition for *nipped*[2], one meaning stood out: "To stop (something) before it can develop or mature." The bird probably would have been severely injured if it had been a few inches to the left or the right. How many times have we been nipped? How many times have we allowed people to stop us! Why do we allow our dreams to be shattered? What is stopping us from developing into the men and women that G-d planned for us to be before the foundation of the world! Psalm 139:14 reads, "I will praise You, for I am fearfully and wonderfully made; Marvelous are Your works, And *that* my soul knows very well." G-d made you in His image. He created you and me. Genesis 1:27 states, "So G-d created man in His *own* image; in the image of G-d He created him; male and female He created them." He has a plan for you and me. He has beset you behind and before! If you have been nipped, you can recover!

> Decree and declare this verse of Scripture from Isaiah 40:28–31:
> "Have you not known?
> Have you not heard?
> The everlasting G-d, the L-RD,
> The Creator of the ends of the earth,
> Neither faints nor is weary.
> His understanding is unsearchable.
> He gives power to the weak,
> And to *those who have* no might He increases strength.

I SEE YOU, AND I KNOW! | 43

Even the youths shall faint and be weary,
And the young men shall utterly fall,
But those who wait on the L-RD
Shall renew *their* strength;
They shall mount up with wings like eagles,
They shall run and not be weary,
They shall walk and not faint."

This bird was beset by G-d Himself. While under the tree on the green grass on that hot day, G-d allowed the bird to regain strength! There is no doubt in my mind that this was an assignment for me to let me know that if He can rescue that bird, he can rescue me!

G-d lets me know that He cares about me beyond what I think.

G-d lets me know that He is omnipresent (He is *everywhere* at the same time).

G-d lets me know that he is omnipotent (He is *Almighty*).

G-d lets me know that He is omniscient (He knows *everything*).

The gentlemen from the wildlife center ended the conversation with me by saying, "This was a very happy ending." I couldn't agree more.

LET'S GO DEEPER!

Beset[1] – to surround from all sides. To set or place (like a ring with jewels).

Isaiah 55:8-9, *"For my thoughts are not your thoughts, Nor are your ways My ways," says the L-RD. For as the heavens are higher than the earth, so are my ways higher than your ways, and My thoughts than your thoughts."*

What are you thinking right now?

_____

_____

_____

_____

Nipped[2] – to stop (something) before it can develop or mature.

How many times have we been nipped?
How many times have we allowed people to stop us – to speak to us negatively.
Why do we allow our dreams to be shattered?
What is stopping us from developing into the person that G-d planned for us to be before the foundation of the world!

He is surrounding us from all sides.
If you have been nipped, you can recover.
When we are in our moments of grief, our moments of disbelief, our moments of unsettling situations and decisions, G-d allows us to regain strength in Him.

Isaiah 40:28-31

"Have you not known? Have you not heard? The everlasting G-D, the L-RD,
The Creator of the ends of the earth, Neither faints nor is weary.
His understanding is unsearchable. He gives power to the weak,
And to those who have no might He increase strength.
Even the youths shall faint and be weary, And the young men shall utterly fall,
But those who wait on the L-RD Shall renew their strength;
They shall mount up with wings like eagles,
They shall run and not be weary,
They shall walk and not faint."

G-d has His Hands upon us. He loves us and cares for us. I encourage each of you to Read the entire 17th Chapter of the Gospel according to John. Here Jesus prays for all Believers starting at verse 20.

Now that you have read John 17, what are your thoughts?

_____
_____
_____
_____
_____
_____
_____
_____

Let me encourage you.

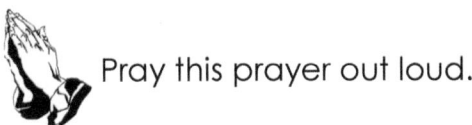 Pray this prayer out loud.

Dear Heavenly Father,

When I think about where You have brought me from, my very soul cries out praises to You. Thank You for sparing my life, my husband's life and for protecting my family, friends, and neighbors. Thank You for caring for me, strengthening me when I am weak, and keeping me in Your loving arms. I am nothing without You. Please help us to be more grateful and thankful with each passing day. And may our praise and our prayers be pleasing to Your ear.

In Jesus' Name – Amen.

CHAPTER 6

YOU CANNOT ESCAPE!

Where can I go from Your Spirit?
Or where can I flee from Your presence?
When I awake, I am still with You.
—Psalm 139:7 & 18b

For the beginning of this chatper, I want to elaborate on Psalm 139, verse 18b first - and I quote,

"When I awake, I am still with You."

This is a powerful and thought provoking statement.

Studies shows over and over how important sleep benefits us. Yet, some of us get very little sleep (me included). Whatever the reason, overtiredness, sickness, pain or discomfort in our bodies, eventually we fall asleep.

How comforting to know after a night of sleep when G-d touches us and awake us, we can still be with Him. Knowing this should prompt in us a "good morning dear Heavenly Father."

As I grow older, I am becoming more intentional about acknowledging G-d immediately upon opening my eyes from sleep. I like to acknowledge Him with a soft voice or sometimes a whisper. I not only say a good morning to G-d the Father, but also our Savior, the L-RD Jesus Christ and the Holy Spirit (herein the Godhead). I believe G-d honors faithfulness and I want to be pleasing in His sight at all times. Yes! *"When I awake, I am still with You."*

How about you? Let's put into practice speaking with our Heavenly Father first thing upon our wakening.

I'm quite sure we have all played the game hide-and-seek at some time in our lives as children. I didn't like that game too much. It's okay to hide, but hearing feet coming closer and closer to where you are hiding is not a good feeling. I don't like anyone or anything chasing me. At the age of thirteen, I ran from a German Shepherd dog that was chasing me and ended up falling down on iron bars and tearing quite a few ligaments in my leg. No matter how much you may run, or where you are at present, you cannot escape G-d. We run from G-d as if He can't see us. Let me let you in on a secret: *shhhh,* "*He can see you.*" Isn't it amazing that a lot of crime happens at night and in the wee hours of the morning, in the dark when no one is looking? Ah, but G-d sees it. There is no darkness in Him at all! The dark is just as light to Him. We read in Jeremiah 23:23–24, *"Am* I a G-d near at hand," says the L-RD, "And not a G-d afar off? Can anyone hide himself in secret places, So I shall not see him?" says the L-RD; "Do I not fill heaven and earth?" says the L-RD. In Psalm 139:12, it says, "Indeed, the darkness shall not hide from You, But the night shines as the day; The darkness and the light *are* both alike to *You,*" and 1 John 1:5 reads, "This is the message which we have heard from Him and declare to you, that G-d is light and in Him is no darkness at all." Don't run from Him. You cannot escape!

Sometimes our feelings are hidden behind a smile so that no one will recognize when we are going through a hard time. We can't hide our feelings from G-d. We don't have to pretend we love Him. He knows that too. There is absolutely nothing that you can hide from G-d. Wow! You always feel better when you get things out in the open. It may hurt a little, or be embarrassing, but what a relief when you no longer hide.

This is why prayer is so important to the life of the Believer. Jesus left a model prayer for us in Matthew 6:9-13 (NKJV).

> "In this manner, therefore pray:
> Our Father in heaven,
> Hallowed be Your name.
> Your kingdom come.
> Your will be done
> On earth as *it is* in heaven.
> Give us this day our daily bread.
> And forgive us our debts,
> As we forgive our debtors.
> And do not lead us into temptation,
> But deliver us from the evil one.
> For Yours is the kingdom and the power and the glory forever.
> Amen."

We should go into prayer with the understanding that He knows what we need. There are no secrets in prayer. Watch out! The L-RD has more to say to you than you have to say to Him.

I would like to end this chapter sharing the song lyrics to "Surprises"[1] by Meleasa Houghton and Israel Houghton. I am reminded quite often that G-d sees and knows ALL THINGS. There are "no surprises" about us that we can hide from Him.

"Where can I go from Your Spirit?
Or where can I flee from Your presence?"
—(Psalm 139:7)

I hope you will take the time to listen to this song.

"Surprises"[1]

From first to last
You knew my days
Future and past
You saw everything
When I would fail
When I would win
When I would need
Grace to start again

Nothing surprises You
Nothing surprises You about me, Jesus
Nothing that I could do
Nothing could separate You from me Oh,
You see me
You know me!
You love me madly

Cover my life
Order my steps
I'll follow Christ?
My answer's yes
Sometimes I'll rise
And sometimes I'll fall
So glad your love is unconditional

Nothing surprises You
Nothing surprises You about me, Jesus
Nothing that I could do
Nothing could separate You from me
Oh, You see me You know me!
You love me madly

And You're not mad at me
You're not mad at me
You're more than enough
Oh You're madly in love with me

And You're not mad at me
You're not mad at me
You're more than enough
Oh you're madly in love with me

No, You're not mad at me
No, You're my Daddy
You're more than enough
Oh You're madly in love with me

You're not mad at me
You're not mad at me
You're not mad at me
More than enough
More than enough
You see me
You know me
You love me madly

LET'S GO DEEPER!

Do you have a prayer life? What is a "prayer life" you may ask. Well, prayer is special. Prayer can go where no one can visit. It's only you and G-d. It's the inner being, your spirit that connects with Him. He already knows our hearts because He is the maker of it. Since we cannot hide anything from Him, prayer becomes an intimate time with Him. You can cry and don't say a word. He sees our tears and know our hurts.

I love this scripture in 2 Corinthians 1:3-5 (NKJV):

> *"Blessed be the G-d, and Father of our L-RD Jesus Christ,*
> *the Father of mercies, and G-d of all comfort, who comforts us in*
> *all our tribulation, that we may be able to comfort those who are in any*
> *trouble, with the comfort with which we ourselves are comforted by G-d.*
> *For as the sufferings of Christ abound in us,*
> *so our consolation also abounds through Christ."*

Prayer is a very important and vital aspect of the Believer. In a relationship, you share and talk about life, work, your fears, your aspirations, etc. There's no difference in prayer. You can share all these things with G-d. The key is "faith" to believe that He hears you.

Do you think G-d hears you? What do you want to say to Him?

_____

_____

_____

_____

Here is another scripture that I have loved over the years when I think about my prayer life. 1 John 5:14-15 (NKJV):

> *"Now this is the confidence that we have in Him, that if we ask anything according to His will, He hears us. And if we know that he hears us, whatever we ask, we know that we have the petitions that we have asked of Him."*

As I stated before, G-d knows what we need and He invites us to talk to him through prayer.

Do you have hope? I have a star of hope. It's true! It's a real star in the sky. Actually if I'm awake between the hours of 3:00 - 5:00 a.m., and the sky is clear, I can see a cluster of stars but sometimes, there is one star that the L-RD will allow me to see. I look for it during my prayer time. When I see it, I smile.

G-d knows the heights He wants you to take. He knows when we have high ambitions and when we need a change in life. So keep reaching for your goals and rise above your circumstances. In prayer, you can share these precious moments with Him. *"But He knows the way that I take, When He has tested me, I shall come forth as gold."* Job 23:10 (NKJV).

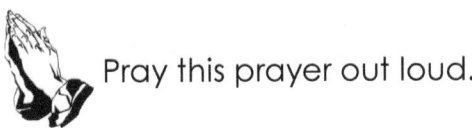

Let me encourage you.

Pray this prayer out loud.

Dear Heavenly Father,

I realize I cannot hide from You. Please forgive me for not trusting You as I should. You hear everything that I say. You see where I go and what I do. I want to be pleasing in Your sight. Help me to be mindful of my surroundings and to be an example for You in my daily walk. Please increase my prayer life and give me the faith to truly believe that with You, all things are possible.

In Jesus' Name – Amen.

CHAPTER 7

I GIVE UP!

Have you ever been so frustrated that you throw your hands up and say, "I give up!" Yes, me too. When we surrender our all to the L-RD, He will begin to work out everything for us. You may not know the exact date, hour, and minute, but trust me, He will make everything right. Please don't take this the wrong way. I am not asking you to give up with no hope in sight. I'm encouraging you to say, "I surrender. I give up *all* to the L-RD. I give Him my life, my thoughts, my husband, my wife, my mother, my father, my sisters, my brothers, my cousins, my nieces, my nephews, my sons and daughters, my grandchildren, my coworkers, and my sisters and brothers in church. I give up trying to fix all of them." We love to fix things, especially people.

I remember in the early years of my marriage, I wanted everything to be perfect. Spotless house, ironed sheets and t-shirts, everything folded to perfection. Mopping and dusting every night so it could look like a magazine picture when we woke up. On one particular day, I called my mother-in-love to find out what my husband's favorite foods were so I could prepare a special dinner for him. Everything was going perfectly, and when he arrived home from work, he said, "Wow! It smells good in here." I was so happy. When he approached the kitchen, I was stirring in one of the pots and tasted the food to make sure it didn't need more seasoning. He saw me as I continued to stir with the same spoon in the pot, and said, "No! Don't put the same spoon back in the pot!" You could only imagine the look on my bewildered face as I already had started stirring again. He said, "Oh my goodness, I'm going to be sick!" The end of this story is that he not only didn't eat any of the food I prepared that night, but it was a long time before he would eat anything else I prepared. I said to myself, "*I give up! I'm not cooking anymore. We will just eat out.*" Of course, you learn as you go along. I never did that again! I had to stop testing food and stirring with the same utensil if I wanted him to eat my food.

How many times have we been frustrated with a situation only to throw up our hands in defeat? We don't have to give up and throw in the towel on life, but we should give everything to the L-RD, especially if it brings hurt feelings, disbelief, or sorrow. You may have experienced not getting along with a coworker or a family member. Give them over to the L-RD. We take on undue stress and pressure to the point where we throw our hands up and become tense, frustrated, disappointed, and the like. It's not always easy to give up and allow someone else to take control. This reminds me whenever I try a new application on the computer, and just can't seem to figure it out, I can call on the help of the experts (or the help desk) and ask a technician to help me resolve the issue. Sometimes, the technician may ask permission to take control of my computer. Once I give permission, I watch the mouse move from point A to point B as the technician attempts to resolve the issue. Most of the time, he or she succeeds. I have encouraging news for you! When we give our situations to the L-RD, He not only takes control, but He *always* resolves the issue. It may not be in the timeframe you want, but trust me, He knows the when, where, how, and why of every situation we are in. When we give Him complete control, we can be assured that He will never make a mistake.

I love the hymnal
"I Surrender All"[1]

All to Jesus I surrender;
all to him I freely give;
I will ever love and trust him,
in His presence daily live.

Refrain:
I surrender all,
I surrender all,
All to Thee, my blessed Savior,
I surrender all.

All to Jesus I surrender;
Humbly at His feet I bow,
Worldly pleasures all forsaken;
Take me, Jesus, take me now.
(Refrain)

All to Jesus I surrender;
Make me, Savior, wholly Thine;
Let me feel the Holy Spirit;
Truly know that thou art mine.
(Refrain)

All to Jesus I surrender;
Lord, I give myself to Thee;
Fill me with Thy love and power;
Let thy blessing fall on me.
(Refrain)

All to Jesus I surrender;
Now I feel the sacred flame.
Oh the joy of full salvation!
Glory, glory, to His name!
(Refrain)

LET'S GO DEEPER!

What does it mean to surrender[2]?
- (1) to agree to stop fighting, hiding, resisting, etc., because you know that you will not win or succeed.
- (2) to give the control or use of (something) to someone else.

When we surrender our lives to Him, that means we depend on Him for every aspect of our life. Sometimes, we only give Him what we want and hold back on the rest but He wants ALL OF YOU, not just part of you.

There are a plethora of scriptures pertaining to surrendering your life to Christ. Here are a few you can write out for your review and study.

Jeremiah 29:11-13

_____

_____

_____

_____

_____

Galatians 2:20

_____

_____

_____

_____

_____

James 4:7

___

___

___

___

___

Matthew 16:24

___

___

___

___

___

Romans 12:2

___

___

___

___

___

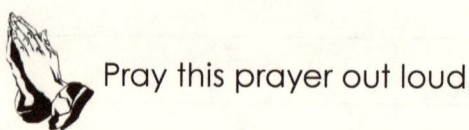

Let me encourage you.

Pray this prayer out loud.

Dear Heavenly Father,

Thank You for Your unfailing love. Please help me when I become impatient and want to throw my hands up. Help me to understand that You are in control of my life. As I surrender my life to You, please help me surrender ALL, not just part of me. Help me to surrender my family and any aspect of my life going forward. I want to surrender my all to You.

Thank You for hearing my prayer.
In Jesus' Name — Amen.

CHAPTER 8

SEARCH ME OUT

Search me, O G-d, and know my heart:
try me, and know my thoughts.
—Psalm 139:23

I have to be honest with you. Just the thought of having someone search me out is not easy. Think about it. If someone says to you, "Okay, I need to know everything about you, so give me a couple of hours so I can do a thorough background check on you. I need to check out where you were born, when you were born, your school records, and so forth." You may agree to this because you think that the person won't find anything wrong. Then you remember that in the fourth grade, you had a fight; in the fifth grade, you stole something; in the sixth grade you failed, and so forth. How would that make you feel?

Psalm 139 was written by King David after the prophet Nathan confronted him about the sin that he had committed with Uriah's wife, Bathsheba (see 2 Samuel, chapters 11 and 12). After receiving word that Bathsheba was expecting, he sent for Uriah to come home and spend time with his wife, hoping that he would enjoy intimacy with her so when Uriah would hear the news that his wife was expecting, he would think that the unborn child is his. But we read in 2 Samuel 11:9–11: "But Uriah slept at the door of the king's house with all the servants of his lord, and did not go down to his house. So when they told David, saying, "Uriah did not go down to his house," David said to Uriah, "Did you not come from a journey? Why did you not go down to your house?" And Uriah said to David, "The ark and Israel and Judah are dwelling in tents, and my lord Joab and the servants of my lord are encamped in the open fields. Shall I then go to my house to eat and drink, and to lie with my wife? As you live, and *as* your soul lives, I will not do this thing." Since David's plan didn't work, He wrote a letter to Joab and sent it by the hand of Uriah. The letter said, "Set Uriah in the forefront of the hottest battle, and retreat from him, that he may be struck down and die" (v.14). So Uriah died in battle, and David arranged it. After the dust had settled and Bathsheba's mourning was over, David brought her to his house. 2 Samuel 11:26–27, "When the wife of Uriah heard that Uriah her husband was dead, she mourned for her husband. And when her mourning was over, David sent and brought her to his house, and she became his wife and bore him a son. But the thing that David had done displeased the L-RD."

King David thought that he had covered all bases. But the L-RD sent the prophet Nathan to David and exposed everything. David did repent, and his sin was forgiven, but he reaped consequences from his actions.

We cannot escape from the watchful eye of G-d.

Of course there are things in our hearts that need to be cleaned out. Even the best of persons have a spot here and there that can be cleaned.

I love to clean, sit back, enjoy the fresh smell of air fresheners, and view the shimmering mirrors. Wear and tear, and the earth elements take a toll even on furniture. No matter how much you clean, there will always be dust and a knick here or there. I remember one time when I was cleaning my glass table and noticed a flaw in the table. I tried to clean it repeatedly, but it was a permanent mark. I didn't remember seeing that spot when we purchased it. Okay, what does this have to do with G-d searching me out and knowing my heart? Well, when we ask G-d to search us out and know our hearts, He will bring to our remembrance very small details that have taken root and been placed on shelves in our hearts. They collect dust and it starts to get crowded. G-d will help you clean the clutter in your heart, such as past hurts and people treating you wrongly for things you may not have had control over. G-d is the maker of our hearts.

In my prayer time, this is one of the prayers I pray daily, asking G-d to search me and clean me through and through. "Search me, O G-d, and know my heart; Try me, and know my thoughts: And see if *there is any* wicked way in me, and lead me in the way everlasting."
(Psalm 139-23-24)

LET'S GO DEEPER!

The following passages of scriptures reminds us and encourages us that G-d wants us to search for Him, seek Him and trust Him totally.

Proverbs 20:27:
*"The spirit of man is the lamp of the L-RD,
Searching all the inner depths of his heart."*

Isaiah 55:6-7:
"Seek the L-RD while He may be found, call upon Him while He is near. Let the wicked forsake his way, and the unrighteous man his thoughts: and let him return to the L-RD, and He will have compassion on him; and to our G-d, for He will abundantly pardon."

Jeremiah 29:13:
"And you will seek Me and find Me, when you search for Me with all your heart."

Ezekiel 34:11:
*"For thus says the L-RD G-d,
"Behold, I Myself will search for My sheep and seek them out."*

Matthew 7:7-8:
"Ask, and it will be given to you; seek, and you will find; knock, and it will be opened to you. For everyone who asks receives, and he who seeks finds, and to him who knocks it will be opened."

After reading these passages of the scriptures, what is it that you want G-d to do for you.

_____

_____

_____

_____

_____

_____

_____

_____

_____

_____

_____

_____

_____

_____

_____

_____

We can't hide our hearts from Him. Remember, He sees and He knows!

Let me encourage you.

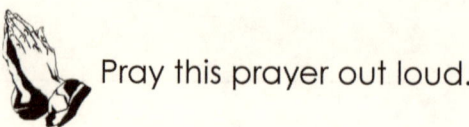 Pray this prayer out loud.

Dear Heavenly Father,

You said in Your Word in Ezekiel 36:26–27, "I will give you a new heart and put a new spirit within you; I will take the heart of stone out of your flesh and give you a heart of flesh. I will put My Spirit within you and cause you to walk in My statutes, and you will keep My judgments and do them." As I seek your Face and call upon You, please heal my broken heart. Where there is hurt, please heal. Where there is sorrow, please comfort. Where there is unforgiveness, please forgive me and allow me to forgive. Please give me a clean heart that I may serve You. I want to be pleasing in Your sight and give You praise all the days of my life.

In Jesus' Name – Amen.

CHAPTER 9

LEAD ME

And lead me in the way everlasting.
—Psalm 139:24

Have you ever played the game pin the tail on the donkey? I don't particularly care for that game only because someone has to blindfold you in order to play the game. Your hands are outstretched, and you are trying to see without seeing. You hear your audience shouting to you, "Move over!" or "You're too far!" or "Closer!" When you remove your blindfold, you can see how far off you are.

When I was a little girl, I remember the song sung quite often in church "Where He lead, me I, will follow, I'll go with Him, with Him, all the way."[1] It's amazing how you can sing a song and not know the true meaning until you grow up. Of course, years later, I realized that we only sang this song's refrain. The words in this song always touched my heart, even at an early age. When we don't allow G-d to lead us, we become blind with seeing eyes. There are numerous passages of Scripture about G-d leading us. Here are only a few.

Psalm 23:2–3 (NIV): "He makes me lie down in green pastures, He leads me beside quiet waters, He refreshes my soul. He guides me along the right paths for his name's sake."

Psalm 25:5 (NIV): "Guide me in your truth and teach me, for you are G-d my Savior, and my hope is in you all day long."

Psalm 31:3 (NIV): "Since you are my rock and my fortress, for the sake of your name lead and guide me."

Isaiah 48:17 (NIV): This is what the L-RD says—your Redeemer, the Holy One of Israel; "I am the L-RD your G-d, who teaches you what is best for you, who directs you in the way you should go."

I want the L-RD to lead me in every area of my life, and over the years, I have tried my best to follow His lead. Sometimes I went my own way only to end up in pain and suffering or regret, but thank G-d for His grace and mercy. This passage of Scripture is worth mentioning time after time: Lamentations 3:22–23 reads, "Through the L-RD's mercies we are not consumed, Because His compassions fail not. They are new every morning; Great is Your faithfulness."

Asking the L-RD to lead you doesn't just involve you. If you are married, or have a family or any type of family relationship, there will be times when you will need to ask the L-RD to lead you to make decisions. Let's go back to "sit", (**stay-in-**touch) with G-d through prayer. As you pray throughout your day, ask the L-RD to lead you in the direction that He wants you to go. I love the story of Moses. He had to depend totally on G-d to help him lead the children of Israel from the wrath of Pharaoh and out of Egypt through the wilderness. Look at this powerful passage of Scripture in Exodus. "And the L-RD went before them by day in a pillar of cloud to lead the way, and by night in a pillar of fire to give them light, so as to go by day and night. He did not take away the pillar of cloud by day or the pillar of fire by night *from* before the people" (Exodus 13:21-22).

Today we have the Holy Spirit to lead and guide us into all truth. So let Him lead you today and in every area of your life. "Show me Your ways, O L-RD; Teach me Your paths. Lead me in Your truth and teach me, For You *are* the G-d of my salvation; On You I wait all the day" (Psalm 25:4–5). Here is another attribute that all of us need to learn at one time or another - to "wait." There is a blessing in waiting. The Scripture reminds us in Philippians 4:6–7, "Be anxious for nothing, but in everything by prayer and supplication, with thanksgiving, let your requests be made known to G-d; and the peace of G-d, which surpasses all understanding, *will* guard your hearts and minds through Christ Jesus" (emphasis mine).

LET'S GO DEEPER!

There are several words I want to point out from this chapter.

The first word is **Lead**[2] – *to go <u>before</u> or <u>with</u> to <u>show the way</u>; <u>conduct</u> or <u>escort</u>:*

From the scriptures given in Chapter 9 and from this definition above, I encourage you to write a prayer, thought or insight.

_____
_____
_____
_____
_____
_____
_____
_____
_____
_____
_____
_____
_____

The next word is **Sit**[3] – *to attend or take part as a visitor or temporary participant.* This definition is different from the one I spoke about in Chapter 2.

In Psalm 1, verse 2-3 it reads *"But his delight is in the law of the L-RD, And in His law he meditates day and night. He shall be like a tree Planted by the rivers of water, That brings forth its fruit in its season, Whose leaf also shall not wither; And whatever he does shall prosper." (NKJV)*

From these verses, I encourage you to write a prayer, thought or insight on how you can "stay-in-touch" **(sit)** with G-d.

_____

_____

_____

_____

_____

_____

_____

_____

_____

_____

_____

The last word I want to point out is **Wait**[4] – (noun) *an act or instance of waiting or awaiting; delay;* (verb) *continue in expectation.*

It's amazing that we pray for G-d to lead us and don't have patience to wait for an answer. I have often heard the statement from sermons that G-d has three answers for you when you come to Him in prayer. Yes. No. Wait. Wait can also means, not now. It doesn't mean it won't come to fruition, you just have to wait for the right time. G-d's timing is always right. He's never late.

There have been many times that I had petitions before the L-RD and was hoping for a quick answer. Most of the time my answers came after a long period. Other times, I set time aside to fast along with prayer because my request was that important to me and I really needed the right answer and the right decision to make.

Waiting is not an easy task, especially if you are a very busy person. We live in a very fast-pace era when you can get a plethora of information from technology with just a keystroke. Cook food in record time and vacuum your floor automatically without a person holding a handle. No wonder we don't have the patience to wait. Here are a few people in the Bible who had to wait for answers.

We read in 1 Samuel, chapter 1 about the wife of Elkanah who was barren. In verses 10-11, we read – *"In her deep anguish Hannah prayed to the L-RD, weeping bitterly. And she made a vow, saying, "L-RD Almighty, if you will only look on your servant's misery and remember me, and not forget your servant but give her a son, then I will give him to the L-RD for all the days of his life, and no razor will ever be used on his head."* The profound part of this story is verse 13, *"Hannah was praying in her heart, and her lips were moving but her voice was not heard."* G-d "sees and knows" and even "hear your hearts cry".

Verse 20, *"So in the course of time Hannah became pregnant and gave birth to a son. She named him Samuel, saying, "Because I asked the L-RD for him."* Samuel grew up in the temple of the L-RD and became a prophet and judge.

Abraham – Waiting for a Promise to Be Fulfilled. *"Then Abraham waited patiently, and he received what G-d had promised"* (Hebrews 6:15). Abraham was promised an heir through his wife Sarah despite her old age.

Joseph – Waiting in Prison for a Purpose. *"You intended to harm me, but G-d intended it for good to accomplish what is now being done, the saving of many lives"* (Genesis 50:20).

What about us today? Please ponder on these encouraging scriptures and then write a prayer and thank G-d for leading you.

Psalm 31:3 (NKJV)
*"For You are my rock and my fortress;
Therefore, for Your name's sake, Lead me and guide me."*

Psalm 143:10 (NKJV)
*"Teach me to do Your will, For You are my G-d;
Your Spirit is good. Lead me in the land of uprightness."*

Proverbs 4:11 (NKJV)
*"I have taught you in the way of wisdom;
I have led you in right paths."*

___

2 Thessalonians 3:5 (NKJV)
*"Now may the L-RD direct your hearts into the love of G-d
and into the patience of Christ."*

___

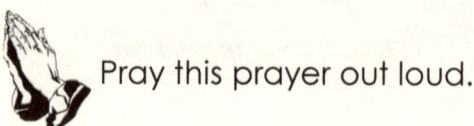

Let me encourage you.

Pray this prayer out loud.

Dear Heavenly Father,

Words cannot express how much I love and adore You. I want to be led by You each day and in every area of my life. Please help me continue to sit (stay-in-touch) with you daily.

As I come to you quietly and with humble submission, please speak to my heart in the stillness and in Your presence.

Please help me to follow You and heed to Your voice when You call. I need patience to wait on You. As I wait, please allow me to be a blessing to my sisters and brothers who may need an encouraging word.

Create opportunities for me to serve as I wait. Allow me to be a beacon of light to encourage someone along the way.

This refrain from the Hymnal "Where He Leads Me" is from my heart to You,

> "Where He leads me I will follow
> Where He leads me I will follow
> Where He leads me I will follow
> I'll go with Him, with Him, all the way!"

In Jesus' Name – Amen.

EPILOGUE

It never cease to amaze me how wonderful our G-d is. The more I reflect on this book the more I realize how much I would need to know that "He Sees me" and He is the only one who truly "Knows" the things that we have gone through, the things He has brought us through and the grace that He has given to us now. He has placed people in our lives for us to be a witness, an encourager and a hope. I thank G-d for the many lives that have been changed after reading this book – your thinking will not be the same after reading Psalm 139 knowing that G-d is watching you every second of the day forever! It's personal and intimate. We don't have to be afraid to be honest with G-d. He already knows!

Psalm 139 is a personal journey that you can refer to and use time and time again for your life. Reflect often, especially when life takes you on a whirlwind of activities and you are caught in the busyness of life.

It's important to understand that we cannot escape G-d's presence. He made us and knows all about us. When we realize that His watchful eye is always on us, hopefully we will begin to think in His direction at all times. We should aspire to be more like Jesus each and every day at home, on our jobs, in our places of worship, and with everyone we meet.

Yes, my friend, G-d sees you, and He knows exactly what you are going through. He wants to lead you on the journey. He knows there will be pitfalls along the way. He loves you so much that His watchful eye will never leave you.

Dear Heavenly Father,

I pray that every person who will take the time to read Psalm 139 and to use this book as a companion, will embrace the scriptures and use it daily in their prayers. May they come to realize that You will never leave them nor forsake them. We need You in every area of our lives, and to that end, we cannot make it without You.

Thank you for hearing my prayer.
In Jesus' Name – Amen.

This section is designed for you to reflect and write.

This section is designed for you to reflect and write.

This section is designed for you to reflect and write.

___

___

___

___

___

___

___

___

___

___

___

___

___

___

___

___

___

___

___

___

This section is designed for you to reflect and write.

ENDNOTES

Prologue:
1. Pelaia, Ariela. The Jewish Spelling of "God" as "G_d". Learn Religions, Jun. 25, 2024, learnreligions.com/ jewish-spelling-of-god-2076772.

Chapter 1: G-d Knows Your Name
1. Call – Chicago Manual Style (CMS):
call. Dictionary.com. *Dictionary.com Unabridged*. Random House, Inc. http://dictionary.reference.com/browse/call (accessed: April 22, 2015 and January 2024).

2. Search – Chicago Manual Style (CMS):
search. Dictionary.com. *Dictionary.com Unabridged*. Random House, Inc. http://dictionary.reference.com/browse/search (accessed: April 16, 2015 and January 2024).

Chapter 2: G-d Knows Where You Sit
1. Sit – Collins English Dictionary – Complete and Unabridged © HarperCollins Publishers 1991, 1994, 1998, 2000, 2003.

2. His Eye is on the Sparrow by Civilla D. Martin, 1905
Charles H. Gabriel, 1905 – Copyright: Public Domain
Hymnsite.com

Chapter 3: G-d Knows When You Rise

1. Rise – Chicago Manual Style (CMS):
   rise. Dictionary.com. *Dictionary.com Unabridged*. Random House, Inc. http://dictionsary.reference.com/browse/rise (accessed: April 16, 2015 and January 2024).

Chapter 4: G-d Understands your Thoughts

1. Afar – Chicago Manual Style (CMS):
   afar. Dictionary.com. *Dictionary.com Unabridged*. Random House, Inc.

2. Thought – Definitions and idiom definitions from Dictionary.com Unabridged, based on the Random House Unabridged Dictionary, © Random House, Inc. 2023.

3. Think – Definitions and idiom definitions from Dictionary.com Unabridged, based on the Random House Unabridged Dictionary, © Random House, Inc. 2023.

Chapter 5: G-d Hands Are Upon Me!

1. Beset – Chicago Manual Style (CMS):
   beset. Dictionary.com. *Dictionary.com Unabridged*. Random House, Inc. http://dictionary.reference.com/browse/beset (accessed: April 22, 2015 and January 2024).

2. Nipped – Random House Kernerman Webster's College Dictionary, ©2010 K Dictionaries Ltd. Copyright 2005, 1997, 1991 by Random House, Inc. All rights reserved.

Chapter 6: You Cannot Escape!

1. Song Title: *Surprises* – License No: 43411, Song No. 17044, Songwriter(s): Israel Houghton, Meleasa Houghton, Israel Houghton – Copyright Line: © 2010
Integrity's Praise! Music (BMI), Sound of the New Breed (BMI) (adm at IntegratedRights.com).

Chapter 7: I Give Up!

1. I Surrender All by Judson W. Van DeVenter, 1896
Copyright: Public Domain – Hymnsite.com

2. Surrender – https://www.britannica.com/dictionary (accessed January 2024)

Chapter 9: Lead Me

1. Where He Leads Me – Words: Ernest W. Blandy, 1890.
Music: John S. Norris, 1890. Copyright: Public Domain.
Faith Publishing House, *Evening Light Songs,* 1949, edited 1987 (243).

2. Lead – Dictionary.com. *Dictionary.com Unabridged.* Random House, Inc. http://dictionary.reference.com/browse/lead (accessed: January 2024).

3. Sit – Dictionary.com. *Dictionary.com Unabridged.* Random House, Inc. http://dictionary.reference.com/browse/sit (accessed: January 2024).

4. Wait – Dictionary.com. *Dictionary.com Unabridged.* Random House, Inc. http://dictionary.reference.com/browse/wait (accessed: January 2024).

ABOUT THE AUTHOR

 **Sheila G. Bullock** is the founder of Women of Worth, Inc. (WOW) Ministries, which helps teenagers, young ladies, and women to find their G-d-given gifts and encourages them to know their worth in G-d.

In 1996, Sheila received her Ministerial License from the Board of Presbytery of the United Holy Church of America, Incorporated.

After serving in various ministries, Sheila worked alongside her husband as First Lady and served in different capacities of the ministry for twenty (20) years. After the retirement of Pastor Bullock, they served under the leadership of Dr. Ronald L. Owens, Senior Pastor of the New Hope Baptist Church in Metuchen, New Jersey. There she served as an Associate Minister, Worship/Choir Leader, Servant Leader for the Women's Ministry and Teen Bible Teacher.

Working with young people and seniors are some of her passions. She has dedicated her life to helping people since her teen years. Now a wife, mother and grandmother of 11, she enjoys spoiling all of them including her own three children and their spouses.

Minister Bullock serves as a Board Member of the New Life Community Development Corporation, a 501(c)3 Organization created to offer services and engage in activities that promotes and support families, friends and the surrounding communities.

Sheila has over thirty years of experience working in the field of Intellectual Property Law. She is the wife of Pastor Nathaniel Bullock, Jr., for over 45 years. Although she leads a very busy life, she manages through her organizational and time management skills. In her "spare time", she enjoys the world of arts and crafts.

Sheila is looking forward to a New Season in her life, one with great expectations and lives to be changed and encouraged through the reading of the Second Edition of, "I See You, and I Know!"

*"Above all, love each other deeply,
because love covers over a multitude of sins.
Offer hospitality to one another without grumbling."*
—1 Peter 4:8-9 (NIV)

We Would Love to Hear from You:
Visit our Website for more information.

Website: www.jetcrawford.com

www.ingramcontent.com/pod-product-compliance
Lightning Source LLC
LaVergne TN
LVHW042245070526
838201LV00088B/29